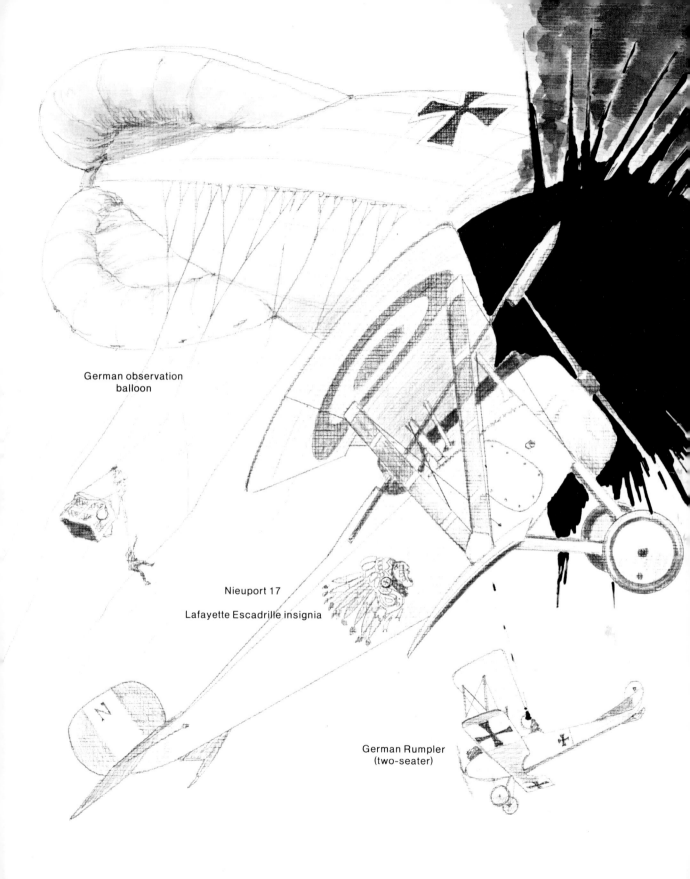

German observation
balloon

Nieuport 17

Lafayette Escadrille insignia

German Rumpler
(two-seater)

Cornerstones of Freedom

The Story of

THE LAFAYETTE ESCADRILLE

By R. Conrad Stein

Illustrated by Len W. Meents

 CHILDRENS PRESS, CHICAGO

Nieuport 11C

German Albatros DII

Library of Congress Cataloging in Publication Data

Stein, R. Conrad.
  The story of the Lafayette Escadrille.

  (Cornerstones of freedom)
  Summary: Describes the war experiences of a group
of American aviators who flew for France in an all-
American squadron for several months before the United
States entered World War I in 1917.
    1. World War, 1914-1918—Aerial operations, French—
Juvenile literature. 2. United States. Army. Aero
Squadron, 103rd—Juvenile literature. [1. World War,
1914-1918—Aerial operations, French. 2. United States.
Army. Aero Squadron, 103rd. 3. Fighter pilots]
I. Title. II. Series.
D603.S73 1983   940.4'4944   82-23508
ISBN 0-516-04660-8   AACR2

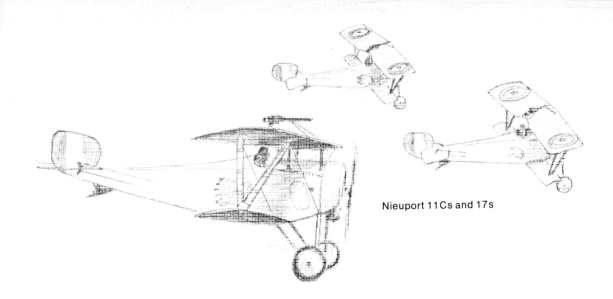

Nieuport 11Cs and 17s

"It was dawn, a Sunday morning in June, 1916. Four of us left our field at Bar-le-Duc [France] to make our regular patrol. We made a long patrol from St. Mihiel to Verdun, getting well into German lines in the early morning."

Those words start a story told by an American flyer named Clyde Balsley. Balsley was one of a handful of Americans who flew for France in the years before the United States entered World War I. He was a member of a very special squadron called the Lafayette Escadrille.

Balsley continues his story, "Across from Hill 305. . . I saw a German plane. Further on I saw more Germans. Then I began to watch my man. It looked like a good chance to pick him off. Diving steeply, I swung to the left to get in line. Down—down. I poised for decision. I would take him!"

But the American pilot's confidence quickly turned to panic. "I held my fire—closer—closer. He was in my sights. I fired once—twice. These were my first and last shots. My machine gun had jammed! I pulled away, but a machine gun opened on my left, another on my right. I was surrounded. I swung in every direction, then through a cloud. Bullets followed.... The linen [on my wings] tore with the bursts. I was about twelve thousand feet up [when] something struck me—like the kick of a mule. I had the sensation as though my leg was shot away and put my hand down to learn if it was still there.... My legs were paralyzed. I fell into a tight spin. It was all over."

Down through the clouds Balsley plunged. His aircraft spun dizzily. He saw the ground racing up to him. The wind screamed in his ears. Balsley heard himself shouting, "Stop yourself. Don't quit." The American pilot struggled with his controls, trying to pull out of the spinning dive. He had fallen to treetop level when his aircraft finally nosed upward. Then Balsley searched the ground for a place to land.

"I was bleeding badly and [felt] faint. Field of green—could I swing for it? I worked my rudder, and turned in for the field. Too late I saw it was

Nieuport 11C

filled with barbed wire. I was landing between the
front lines and the reserves.

"Wheels in the wire, [my airplane] turned over
and crashed. Gasoline was soaking me. I broke my
belt and dropped out. Legs still paralyzed, afraid of
fire, I tried to get to my knees. No hope. Caught onto
the weeds, dragging myself along like a dog with a
broken back. A burst of dust in the field, no sound.
My ears were gone from that terrific dive.
[Artillery shells] dropped all around me. A direct hit
on the ship. The shelling stopped. Four French
soldiers crawled out of their trench, caught hold of
me and dropped me down. I had made my last flight
for France."

Clyde Balsley's story is typical of the wild and savage combat fought by airmen during World War I. Still, young men from all over Europe dreamed of becoming combat pilots.

World War I ranks second only to World War II as the bloodiest conflict fought in modern times. In just four years, some 30 million men were killed or wounded. Ancient Europe never fully recovered from the blows dealt by this awful war.

The war broke out in 1914. European leaders believed it would be short. Under a blazing August sun, young men from Germany and Austria marched bravely off to battlefronts to fight against young men from France, Great Britain, and Belgium. The generals on both sides told the men they would be home by Christmas. But the generals' minds were locked on ancient concepts of battle. The world had entered a new machine age. Weapons of the new age included machine guns and fast-firing artillery. Those weapons had never been used in a major war. The new weapons killed ground troops in astonishing numbers.

By early 1915, the generals' plans for a quick victory had faded. Instead, the nightmare of the trenches began. Bogged-down troops dug lines of deep ditches stretching from the North Sea to Switzerland. Curled in front of the ditches were rolls of barbed wire. In some places along the six-hundred-mile battlefront, only the length of a football field separated the two forces. In the mud and mire of that long trench line, the youth of Europe slowly bled to death.

But in the air, a totally different sort of war developed.

The governments of the warring powers were shocked by the losses suffered on the front. They feared their people would refuse to support the war. So the governments created heroes: the pilots who buzzed through the skies in their flying machines. Heroes always seem to make war more popular. A poster for the British Royal Flying Corps announced: "War in the air recalls the olden times, when knights rode forth to battle and won honor and glory by their deeds of personal heroism." Pilots were heralded as the "New Cavalry," or the "Knights of the Air."

Newspapers joined the campaign to glamorize the role of World War I pilots. It was easy to portray flyers as heroes. They fought in the clean blue skies, high above the dirt and gore of the trenches. Most of them were young and handsome, and they had grown up in wealthy families. Before the war, most "flying machines" had been playthings for the very rich.

Both sides singled out successful pilots as special heroes. When a pilot shot down a certain number of enemy planes (usually five), he was called an "ace."

Aces were idolized by their countrymen. Newspapers published their life stories. They received gold watches and cash gifts from large corporations. Star-struck girls dreamed of marrying ace pilots. Boys studied the records of their favorite pilots the way boys today memorize batting averages of baseball players. One German ace on leave discovered that he was being followed everywhere he went by a twelve-year-old boy who "knew the dates of all my victories."

In Europe, the new knights of the air became as famous as the old kings and queens. Newspapers called France's Georges Guynemer the "Winged Sword of France." Guynemer had fifty-four victories (or kills) when his plane vanished into a cloud and never emerged. Historians believe that Guynemer crashed into the trench line, where artillery chewed up his plane and his body. But one French newsman wrote: "He flew so high he could not come down again." British ace Mick Mannock had nightmares about crashing in a burning plane. He overcame his fears, however, and made seventy-three kills. Finally, he was shot down by ground fire. Before the crash, Mannock's plane burst into flames. Germany's most-celebrated pilot was Manfred von

Fokker Dr. 1

Richtofen

Richthofen. With eighty kills, he was World War I's ace of aces. Richthofen was from an old Prussian family and held the title of baron. In the early days of the war, pilots were allowed to paint their planes any color they wished. Richthofen chose to paint his plane a startling red. His enemies called Richthofen the "Red Baron."

Hoping to join this cavalcade of heroes were many young Americans. But when the European war broke out, President Woodrow Wilson declared the United States to be neutral. Still, most Americans sympathized with France and the Western Powers. Hundreds of "Yanks" (Americans) joined the French Foreign Legion so they could take part in what was being called "The Great War." Many others joined volunteer ambulance units. Several Americans who were serving in the Foreign Legion or in ambulance units asked to become flyers.

At first, the French generals were reluctant to let Americans fly their precious aircraft. But finally, the French saw an advantage to organizing an American Flying squadron. France and Great Britain hoped to persuade America to join the war. So, reasoned the French, a group of American pilot-heroes could make the French cause more popular with the American people. A French official named Sillac wrote: "The United States would be proud . . . that certain of her young men, acting as did Lafayette, would come to fight for France and for civilization. The resulting sentiment could have but one effect — to turn the Americans in the direction of the Allies."

On April 17, 1916, an all-American flying squadron was formed with seven pilots. At first the unit was called the *Escadrille Américaine*. But Germany complained to Washington that a unit with such a name violated America's neutrality. So the name was changed to the *Lafayette Escadrille*. In French the word *escadrille* means squadron. The Marquis de Lafayette was a famous French general who had helped the American colonists defeat Great Britain during the Revolutionary War. Now American flyers could believe they were returning the help Lafayette once gave their country.

Certainly the flyers of the Lafayette Escadrille were dedicated to the cause of France. They believed that France was fighting for all of Western civilization. An American named Jim McConnell explained why he wanted to join the Escadrille: "The more I saw the splendor of the fight the French were fighting, the more I felt like what the British call... a shirker. So I made up my mind to go into aviation."

Like the European flyers, most of the Americans were young and came from wealthy families. William Thaw had been born in Pittsburgh, where his father owned several banks. He dropped out of

William Thaw

Victor E. Chapman

Raoul Lufbery

Yale to fly for France. Thaw later became the squadron leader. Victor E. Chapman's great-great-grandfather was John Jay, the first chief justice of the United States Supreme Court. Chapman became a daredevil pilot who would plunge into a fight even if he were outnumbered two or three to one. Raoul Lufbery was a world traveler who had been born in France and then emigrated to the United States. Because he spoke the French language, "Luf" became the most popular American flyer among the French people. He took the war very personally and flew each mission as if he wanted to destroy Germany all by himself.

The unit did have at least one flyer whose background was less than distinguished. Bert Hall had been born in Missouri "or somewhere in Kentucky," as he later wrote. Almost forty years old, Hall was driving a taxicab in Paris when the war broke out. He enlisted in the French army, but asked to become an airman after five muddy months in the trenches. Hall told his superiors that he was an experienced pilot. In truth, he had never been near enough to an airplane to touch one. Nevertheless, when a French officer asked to see him fly, Hall climbed confidently into the cockpit. A ground crewman started the engine. Suddenly the plane skidded across the runway like "a drunken duck." Hall wrecked the plane and the French officer was furious. Still, the officer allowed Hall to enter pilot training. He admired Hall's spirit.

The French people loved the men of the Lafayette Escadrille. They admired the Americans' humor and their energy. Many service outfits kept dogs and cats as pets. But the Lafayette Escadrille's pets were two lion cubs they had bought from a circus. The men enjoyed wrestling with the young lions on the grass near their airstrip. They called the two beasts Whiskey and Soda.

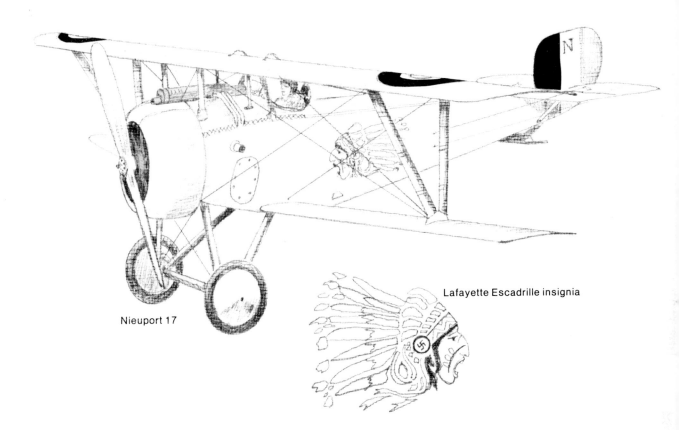

Nieuport 17

Lafayette Escadrille insignia

Pilot training during World War I was dangerous. It sometimes seemed that as many men were killed during training as were killed in combat. At the start of the war, aviation was only a decade old. The men of the Escadrille flew French-built planes. Some of them were not much better than the flying machines flown by the Wright brothers. The planes were made from tubes and canvas held together by wire. The engines on the flimsy craft were underpowered. "When we tried to fly into the teeth of a wind, we found ourselves standing still," wrote one World War I pilot.

Managing to get the primitive planes airborne was a difficult task, especially for a beginning pilot. Escadrille member Victor Chapman described one of his first takeoffs: "The machine left the ground almost immediately, and I had to hold it down to keep headway. Then it began to buck, squirm, wriggle. It slid off to the right, to the left, took a short plunge downward, and then attempted to rear. The earth, a scrawny tree or two, looked near and menacing."

Once airborne, a pilot had to worry constantly about his engine's performance. A leak in the fuel system could send gasoline splashing onto a red-hot engine block. The pilot of a two-seater wrote: "Fire is our third passenger." There were other hazards. If a plug popped out of an engine, oil would squirt out and the engine and the propeller would lock solid. Then the aircraft would plunge to the earth, carrying the helpless pilot with it. At the time the Escadrille was formed, few pilots used parachutes. They were considered unmanly for use by "knights of the air."

The skies over the trenches were an entirely new

battleground. Few military men had ever dreamed that an air war would be fought.

The great French general Napoleon Bonaparte once said, "He who holds the high ground will win." From the high ground, a military leader can observe the troop movements of his enemy. In World War I, generals quickly learned that airplanes could give them a bird's-eye view of their opponents. In the fall of 1914, French scout planes spotted massive German troop movements along the Marne River. Because of those aerial reports, French General Joseph Galliéni knew the Germans were preparing to attack. So Galliéni launched his own attack, and that attack saved the city of Paris.

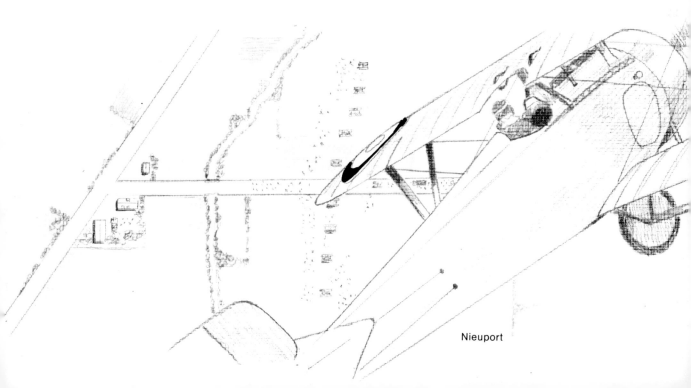

Nieuport

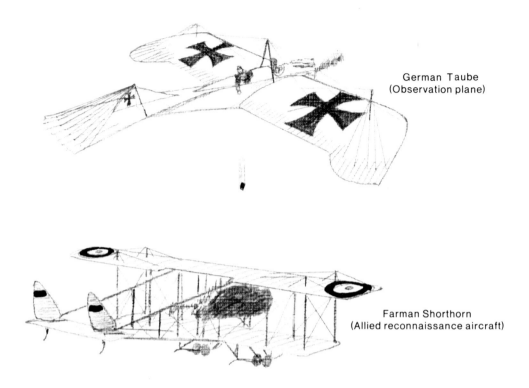

German Taube
(Observation plane)

Farman Shorthorn
(Allied reconnaissance aircraft)

Soon both sides tried to crowd the skies with observation aircraft. Most of those craft were clumsy two-seaters or balloons that hung lazily in the sky. Naturally, the observation aircraft made tempting targets. Pilots began shooting pistols, rifles, and shotguns at each other. One French flyer complained that a German had thrown a brick at him while both were soaring high in the clouds. Finally, a Frenchman attached a machine gun to his two-seater and shot down a German aircraft. After that, the military geniuses created the ultimate airborne weapon—a machine gun synchronized to fire bullets between the whirling blades of a propeller.

In the air as well as in the trenches, the machine gun became the war's most deadly weapon. Aircraft with machine guns that could fire through their propellers gave rise to the fighter plane. The mission of the fighter plane was to drive enemy aircraft out of the sky.

Combat between fighter planes became wild and dizzying. Planes desperately locked in battle were said to be *dogfighting*. Dogfights could rage high in the clouds or as low as treetop level. Fighter pilots developed favorite tricks to shoot down opponents. Baron von Richthofen liked to drop on his enemy "from out of the sun" so his opponent could not see him. A British airman described the terror of being caught from behind by an enemy fighter plane: "You feel naked and helpless.... The panic seeps through your pores...everything seems unreal ...and then you hear the guns hacking. All I can do at the controls is...summon every trick I know ...swerving erratically from side to side so the [German] does not have a steady target. It is a harrowing, execrable ordeal."

Using fighter planes, the European powers struggled to achieve what generals today call *air supremacy*. That means total command of the air over a particular front. With air supremacy, slow-flying aircraft can scout out troop movements without fear of enemy planes.

While the Germans and the Western Allies fought for air supremacy, the Lafayette Escadrille completed its training. At first, the squadron served in a quiet sector at an air base called Luxeuil. It was there that a member of the Escadrille scored the squadron's first kill. On May 18, 1916, Kiffin Rockwell was returning from patrol. His plane had engine trouble and was sputtering badly. Suddenly Rockwell spotted a German two-seater observation plane. Ignoring the sputtering engine, Rockwell gave chase. This was Rockwell's first patrol. He had never before fired his machine gun. Rockwell surprised the German from behind and fired a short machine-gun burst. Smoke puffed out of the enemy plane, and it nosed down and plunged to the earth.

The entire squadron was proud of that first victory. Fellow pilot Jim McConnell wrote, "He [Rockwell] had a great welcome. All Luxeuil smiled upon him—particularly the girls. But he couldn't stay to enjoy his popularity. The Escadrille was transferred to the Verdun sector."

Verdun. The battle for the French city of Verdun

raged for nine months. Waves of ground troops were ordered "over the top" of their trenches and sent charging into the certain death of blazing machine guns. Artillery shells turned the ground into something more forbidding than the face of the moon. Almost one million men—both German and French—lost their lives on the fields of Verdun.

In the skies above Verdun, both sides fought savagely to achieve air supremacy. To Verdun the Germans moved their best planes and their most-accomplished ace pilots. Against this awesome enemy flew the new and inexperienced Lafayette Escadrille.

All American planes are Nieuport 11s and 17s

All German planes are Albatros DIIs

The first American patrol over Verdun took off with seven aircraft. Immediately, the patrol was attacked by swarms of Germans. "It was near being my last patrol," wrote Bert Hall. "The sky seemed full of German planes.... We twisted and turned and dived and slipped and acrobatted around madly. Several times I was so close to my antagonists that I could see their faces quite plainly. Finally, I turned over on my back and went down in a spin, as if I had been hit. Two of them followed me.... When my altimeter registered fifteen hundred feet, I noticed that the Germans had given me up as a goner."

Miraculously, all the Americans returned safely from their first patrol. However, the wings and fusilages of their aircraft were peppered with bullet holes.

During their first week in the skies over Verdun, the Escadrille scored two victories. In the United States, newspapers claimed they were the greatest pilots in the air. In France, the Yanks were praised as heroes. But even heroes die.

Victor Chapman was the boldest member of the Lafayette Escadrille. He once wrote home that he fought so fiercely because he was fighting "for the cause of humanity, the most noble of all causes."

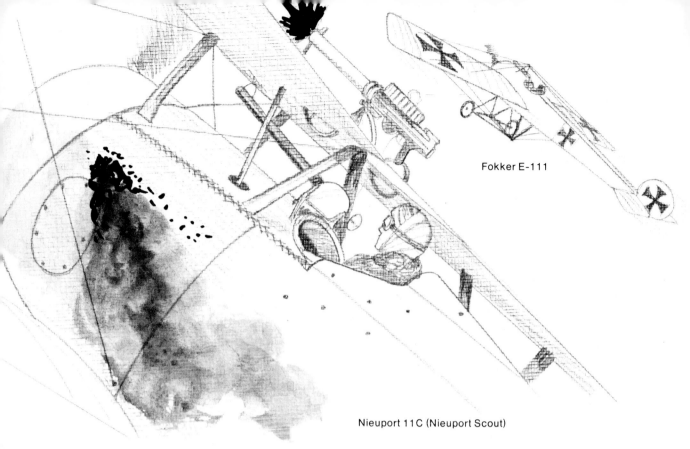

Fokker E-111

Nieuport 11C (Nieuport Scout)

Many of his friends believed Chapman was too brave for his own good. One morning he disobeyed orders by leaving his formation and attacking a German fighter group. He emerged from that battle with a bullet-ridden airplane and a nasty head wound. A week later, with a heavy bandage wrapped around his forehead, Chapman charged five German Fokker aircraft. Victor Chapman was shot down, becoming the first American air casualty of World War I.

While serving at Verdun, the Lafayette Escadrille won the respect of enemy flyers. The great German ace Oswald Boelcke gave this account of his first meeting with the Americans: "I . . . was loafing around the field when I suddenly heard the sound of machine guns and saw [a French plane] attacking one of our planes. The German landed safely. 'The devil is loose at the front,' he told me all out of breath. 'There are six Americans out there. . . . I plainly saw the flag on the fusilage. They are very aggressive and fly far to our side of the lines.' ''

Oswald Boelcke was one of Germany's leading aces. He was also known for his sense of humor. He continued his story: "I decided to go up and give the Americans a welcome. They were probably expecting it. Politeness demanded it. . . . I approached one and said hello with my machine gun. He seemed to be a beginner. But luck foiled me. My [machine gun] jammed. While I was trying to remedy the trouble, the other five Americans attacked me. . . . I maneuvered by tilting my machine to the left and letting it drop. A few hundred yards and I righted it. But they still followed. I repeated the maneuver and flew back to camp. I last saw the Americans resuming their patrol along the front."

In August of 1916, the Escadrille was transferred back to the field at Luxeuil. It was there that Raoul Lufbery scored his fifth kill. This made "Luf" the squadron's first ace.

Strangely, Lufbery had almost failed pilot training. He had a heavy hand at the controls and lacked the "feel" to be a great pilot. But Lufbery, who had been born in France, had an intense hatred for his enemy. On the ground he was a loner who liked to pick mushrooms in the forest. In the air he fought a one-man war. His grim determination enabled "Luf" to score seventeen victories, making him the highest-ranking ace of the Lafayette Escadrille.

As the war-torn months dragged on, the Escadrille suffered more casualties. Kiffin Rockwell was the second squadron member killed in action. Ironically, Rockwell's plane crashed less than a mile from the spot where he had scored the squadron's first kill. Other Americans were killed, wounded, or captured. But there was always a long list of replacements waiting to join the squadron.

One replacement was a shy, blond youth named Edmond Genet. His great-great-grandfather was Citizen Genet, a Frenchman who was a hero in the American Revolutionary War. Genet was a sensitive young man, appalled by the suffering and death he saw around him. Like many soldiers, he had a puzzling belief that he would not survive the war. In a letter to his mother, Genet wrote: "I'd rather die as an aviator over the enemy's lines than find a nameless shallow grave in the infantry."

On April 16, 1917, Genet took off with Raoul Lufbery to fly a routine patrol. His plane was hit by ground fire over the German line. Genet crashed and was killed. At the time of his death, his country was at war. President Wilson had declared that "the world must be made safe for democracy." On April 6, 1917, the United States declared war on Germany and the Central Powers. Edmond Genet was the first American aviator killed after the declaration of war.

America's entry into the war meant the end of the Lafayette Escadrille. The squadron's pilots were ordered into regular United States air units. Many Escadrille members became teachers for new American pilots. One new pilot was Eddie Rickenbacker. He scored an astonishing twenty-six victories in just two months to become America's greatest ace.

The Layfayette Escadrille existed for almost twenty months. The squadron was composed of twelve to fifteen pilots. Counting replacements, thirty-six Americans served in the Escadrille. The squadron as a whole shot down fifty-seven enemy planes.

Other American aviators also served with the French before their country entered the war. In all, 267 Americans volunteered to become pilots, and 180 saw combat. Those men served with different French units and were collectively called the Lafayette Flying Corps. The American volunteers suffered great losses. Fifty-one were killed in action.

On a May morning in 1918, Raoul Lufbery was walking along on the grass near his airstrip. Suddenly he heard the high-pitched whine of motors. He looked into the sky and saw an inexperienced American pilot dueling a German two-seater. The American had foolishly shot off all his ammunition at long range. Now he was at the German's mercy. Lufbery raced to his plane to come to the American's aid. In the ensuing dogfight, Lufbery's aircraft burst into flames. While his comrades on the ground watched in horror, the plane looped over on its back and Lufbery fell out. His body plunged into a village near the airfield. Every member of his squadron rushed to the village. One of them was Eddie Rickenbacker. "We arrived at the scene less than thirty minutes after he had fallen," Rickenbacker later wrote. "Already loving hands had removed his

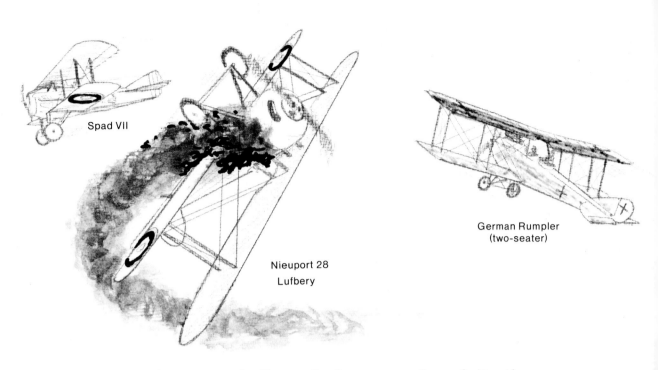

Spad VII

Nieuport 28
Lufbery

German Rumpler
(two-seater)

body to the town hall, and there we found it, the charred figure entirely covered with flowers from nearby gardens."

The most beloved hero of the Lafayette Escadrille was dead. But in war, even heroes die.

Most of the Americans who died flying for France now rest in a cemetery near the French city of Versailles. In the cemetery stands the Lafayette Escadrille Memorial Chapel. The chapel was dedicated on the Fourth of July, 1928. Etched into the walls are the words of English poet Richard Le Gallienne:

France of the many lovers, none than these
Hath brought you love of an intenser flame. . .
Their golden youth they gave, and here are laid
Deep in the arms of France for whom they died.

About the Author

R. Conrad Stein was born and grew up in Chicago. He enlisted in the Marine Corps at the age of eighteen, and served for three years. He then attended the University of Illinois, where he received a Bachelor's Degree in history. He later studied in Mexico and earned a Master of Fine Arts degree from the University of Guanajuato.

The study of history is Mr. Stein's hobby. Since he finds it to be an exciting subject, he tries to bring the excitement of history to his readers. He is the author of many other books, articles, and short stories written for young people.

About the Artist

Len Meents studied painting and drawing at Southern Illinois University and after graduation in 1969 he moved to Chicago. Mr. Meents works full time as a painter and illustrator. He and his wife and child currently make their home in LaGrange, Illinois.